# Enlightened Quotes

By

Lens Georges

A Molding Messengers Publication

Enlightened Quotes

Copyright © 2022 by Lens Georges

All rights reserved. Printed in the United States of America. No part of this book may be used or reproduced in any manner whatsoever without written permission except in the case of brief quotations embodied in critical articles or reviews.

For information about permission to reproduce selections from this book, Write to Molding Messengers, LLC 1728 NE Miami Gardens Drive, Suite #111, North Miami Beach, FL, 33179 or email Info.Staff@MoldingMessengers.com
www.MoldingMessengers.com

Library of Congress Control Number: 2022910318

Print ISBN: 979-8-218-01413-1

eBook ISBN: 979-8-218-01414-8

A Molding Messengers Publication

# Enlightened Quotes

By

Lens Georges

A Molding Messengers Publication

There's nothing like the love God gives us. Through every obstacle & trial He comes through and always reminds you that we are not by ourselves. He always has his hands on you to guide and protect us. Sometimes we all feel like giving up, but He comes through in a mysterious way saying everything is going to be alright, stay strong. That Devil tries to put a hold on you and God grabs you back. He always tells you to have faith and be strong. Can't let that Devil win that battle!

---

The Devil tries to attack you so much. It's not because God doesn't love us, it's because the enemy knows what we carry on our shoulders. When we continue to have faith and God comes through and takes those burdens off our shoulders, it feels good. Sometimes you have to worship when it's not all good. It takes more faith to worship when it doesn't make sense. Don't let the enemy hold you up and break you down. We are stronger than the enemy. We're undefeated worshipers. God can heal you no matter what we've done, we just have to have faith because the love of God will make no sense. God's love reaches down in the most broken places and He comes and save you from whatever we're going through.

The Devil wants you to think that because you keep struggling with the same things, that God wants to get rid of us. When we have that moment of being faithless, He is faithful! He won't deny you because we are still his child. We don't always have the answers, but God is right there with us. We've come too far in life to give up on whatever obstacle that the Devil is trying to place in front of us.

---

There are so many people fighting demons. There are people fighting depression and I pray Jesus places his hands on whoever is in that sunken place. I pray that Jesus will help them come out on the other side and be great. It's so much going on this world so much evil it can cause you to steer away from Jesus, we have to keep our faith stronger than before. I try to bring light with so much darkness and negativity. Can't stay dark forever the light has to shine on you one day. Stay strong and have faith.

---

Most of the times our spirit is willing, but our flesh is telling you something different. The best way to conquer that is with prayer. Prayer is the power that we need because the enemy is counting on you to fail. Don't let the enemy drag you with a burden on your shoulder. Keep fighting him. Prayer and faith will beat Him and knock those burdens off your shoulders anytime of the day. When the Devil tries to take your piece, keep your joy.

---

If God, did it before, He will make a way again. He works miracles. It's a great feeling knowing He has our backs through any journey and obstacle. Prayer is a powerful thing. We serve an amazing God that continues to show you He is almighty and the Devil can't block our blessings.

---

There are plenty of times where the Devil is going to tell you to give up, but in the other ear God will be telling you don't give up. He has his hands on you When we fall God is right there to pick you back up. Don't let the Devil hold you hostage, capturing your happiness and freedom. Shake Him off and continue to have faith and pray.

---

The Devil never saw you coming out and being stronger, but here we are! The Devil thought He could try to put you through obstacles and throw trials and tribulations at you, not knowing you're a child of God. The enemy has been trying you all year, not knowing that you're strong and you're always going to come out stronger than before, because you have God on your side. God has plans for you that the enemy can't get in between. The Devil couldn't break you and God stands ten toes down with you.

---

Don't dwell on what you lost in life, instead be blessed and focus on what you have. God won't bless you on what you lost, he'll focus on now and bless you with what you have now. Your destiny is not in anyone's hands but God. Remember when God delivers you out of something toxic, He also delivers you to something greater.

---

Praise God for all He has done for you and continues doing for you in life. Don't wait for trouble to praise Him and thank him. Praise and thank Him every chance you get. We serve an amazing God. You have to continue having faith even when you're not getting the answers you need at the time. Trust in him. Know that he'll find a way to answer your prayers.

No matter how difficult it might be in life, you always have to continue fighting and having faith. Faith and prayer are powerful. Continue to get through those obstacles the Devil tries to throw at you. God has your back and I pray He continues to shield and guide you through those obstacles.

---

We worship an incredible God. There are times in life you may sit back and think on how God worked his miracles and blessed you in a situation or out of a situation. All I can say is God is good. He deserves all the praise and worship. In this life we live, we can't do this alone. We need God by our side, blessing and protecting us.

---

He continues to watch over us. Sometimes that Devil plays tricks on you. He often tries to make you lose your faith and make you lose your trust in God. Don't let that Devil play that trick on you. God is here for you and He continues to work his power in your life. The power of prayer is very strong. Keep the faith and continue keeping God first.

Our God is a righteous God. Give thanks for all He has done and continues to do. Whatever we're going through I know He is going to get you through. Never lose faith in him, you will make it through. Always praise God for what He has done and continues to do in your life; for He is a great God that continues to work wonders in your life.

---

The Devil comes in your life at times, trying to test you to see how strong your faith is. When your faith is stronger than the Devil there's nothing the Devil can do because our God is an incredible God. He will continue protecting and shielding you from evil. He hears our silent tears. You can't let the Devil win the battle. I know you won't let Him win.

---

The Devil might win some rounds, but He will not win the fight. The battles God gets you through is what makes you who you are. We always come out stronger and God always finds a way to prevail you over the Devil. He is going to make sure we get our miracles and our blessings.

It's always a blessing to receive another day of life. Somewhere in the world, someone right now did not receive a chance to see another day. Be grateful and thankful for that blessing. I continue to thank God for what He has done and continue to do in our lives.

---

It's the hurdles and obstacles we go through in life where the Devil tries to place roadblocks; however, with this amazing God we serve He always finds a way to detour us out and guides us to the right and path. Don't let the Devil win the battle fight through it and keep your faith in God. With Him besides you, you can overcome any outcome.

---

It's so much to be grateful and thankful for. There's nobody greater than him. We live in an evil world, and we can't take this life God has given us for granted. We might be going through some struggles right now, but don't let the Devil take your mind and spirit. He hates when we praise our incredible God. God says to trust him. Put your trust and faith in God and watch Him be your savior. He wants you to trust him. He is an amazing God that works wonders.

---

Give praise for what God has done and continues to do in your life. No matter with all the trauma in our life or even the blessings, God will always make a way. Trust Him and have faith. Don't try and do things by yourself let Him into your life. Let Him love you at your darkest hours. He is the king, our almighty our savior, our protector.

---

Father God, we need you now like never before. In a world full of hate and evilness. We need you, God, to continue watching over us, protecting us. Don't get lost in the corrupted world trying to find yourself. The Devil is going to try to steer you the wrong direction. Continue to have faith. When you have God in the driver seat steering you, it doesn't matter what the Devil does He can't steer you into the wrong direction. The Devil shall not prosper. The power of faith is amazing when you have Him steering you.

There's no problem that happens that God can't get you through. We going to keep fighting, because the fight is never over. God has the final say. We serve God and the Devil has no say so in these battles. Don't focus on how hard the Devil tries to work against you, He will be denied access. Praise our powerful God through the good and the bad.

---

God always has an answer for you. You can depend on the almighty to come through with an answer. Prayer is really big. God listens to our prayers, and he'll change things, so continue having faith. He is a powerful God. These are trying times, and everyone is fighting some battles in life. It's an evil world out here and the Devil comes in all forms and shapes to try to test us. What He doesn't know is we've been battle tested and we have an amazing God that's working in our favor.

---

Continue appreciating the people around you, be thankful for life and counting your blessings. Stop complaining about things that don't go your way. It's always a blessing waking up and getting another chance at life every day. It might not go your way at the time, but God hears you He does his best work in the dark.

---

Give the highest praise for God blessing you to see another day in life. Every single day should be treated as a gift, a lot of people didn't make it. With so much negativity in this world, it's so much to be grateful and thankful for. It's just a blessing knowing you praise an amazing God that continues to amaze and bring you through and out of any challenge in life.

---

Praise and worship are a powerful move of faith. God will catch you on whatever you're doing, don't be afraid to fall. Don't let the Devil place doubts in your life. Stay away from the bad energy. Your life, your mind, and your spirit are a garden; be careful of who you let plant any negative seeds in your garden. There are some people who don't want to see you blessed. Focus on the positive and let God keep elevating you for the best.

Those trials and troubles make you stronger, and it feels much better when God gets you through them. It feels good when you keep the faith, continue in prayer, and see how God has an amazing blessing for you. Prayer and faith can take you out those places the Devil tries to keep you in.

---

I just want to thank the incredible God we praise for everything He has done and continues to do for us. Sometimes when you think you're down and out, and the enemy has you in the corner and you can't do nothing about it. Our amazing God comes through and show you why He is our savior and how incredible He is. The enemy can't keep you down without God having something to say about it.

---

Don't care what the Devil promised you. Don't give up and fall for his trap. Don't focus on your circumstances, continue sending those praises up to God. When the praises go up to God. He really makes those blessings come down. Your praise crushes the enemy. Have prayer and patience, sometimes the blessings God has prepared for you takes time, wait on it! We serve an amazing God that comes through in those times when you think it's impossible.

---

This world and the people in it are broken and fractured, don't let it break you! Let God remove those demons off you. Let Him cleanse you off that bad spirit or the bad people that's around you. Those demons come in all shapes and forms. God will continue to steer you and take control and keep those spirits away.

---

God did not create you to carry those burdens alone. He is our defense. Sometimes you don't know where it's coming from the burden that's holding you down, but you got to stay in the fight God won't leave you like that to fight those battles by yourself. Don't matter what the Devil does always have to keep faith and praise God. That Devil wants you to believe just because you got caught in that storm that you're going to give up. What He doesn't know is that you're going to make it through that storm because your faith is bigger than your fear.

He is a powerful God that continues to guide you through the stormy weather in life. He detours you from the route the Devil attempts you to go through. It's a blessing knowing God has our back whenever the Devil tries to make his move in your life. Prayer and worship are everything with all the craziness going around. All you have is faith and prayer. You can't let the Devil get that chance or enjoyment of getting close to you. With everything you go through, you must owe it all to God for pulling you out.

---

When you're lost and need help, just hold on and be strong. Praise God even in your darkest time. The storm won't last, it's just a test you're going through. Be strong and hold on, God has your back. Praise Him through everything for He has done and continues to do blessing us.

---

Sometimes the Devil will put you in a position that is uncomfortable and have you thinking there's no way out. God will come through and show you it's always a way out of those obstacles. You have the authority you resist the Devil. The Devil is not attacking you because you're weak,

He is attacking you because of your purpose. He knows you're blessed and highly favored.

---

The Devil been busy lately, but I can't let Him win the battle. When we fall, we get right back with God holding you up. Keep a strong faith and continue those prayers whatever that's weighing heavy on your heart pray about it. Don't let that Devil take your joy don't give Him an inch of your joy.

---

Keep your soul cleansed with nothing but good energy around you. Continue sending those praises up and keeping faith. Sometimes life doesn't make sense all the time. Even though it might not make sense right now, God will come in and solve that problem and put that puzzle together and it will all make sense. Keep God at the center. Don't let your pride keep you from being blessed.

---

God is good no matter what we're going through. Always stay focused. You can't let the enemy knock your off you track. Through the bad and good He finds a way to come through. Those stormy days the Devil tries to forecast on you don't last; God always comes through and shine that sun and clear the storm on those days the Devil try to take over.

---

We serve an amazing God. Every time the Devil attacks, I know God is about to do something. The battle doesn't belong to you, it belongs to him. All He asks is to have faith in Him and continue to worship Him while He leads you to victory.

---

Be appreciative. There is nothing too hard for Him He is in control of every situation. Only God can take a negative and turn it too good. There's always a way! Don't let the negativity hold you down. The Devil will not prosper. Keep the positive energy around you and be grateful for the people around you with positive vibe and energy.

---

Thank Him for what He has done for you and continues to do for you. There's nobody better, stronger, or greater than our God. That breakthrough and blessing you've been waiting on will come in due time. Prayers do work miracles.

---

Every day isn't perfect. Life isn't perfect. We all aren't perfect, but God continues to guide & protect you from those bad energy. Everyday it's a struggle and a battle when you have the enemy trying to pull you down in life. The love of God is so real, when you think you're down in a sinking place, He comes through and pull you up from those enemies trying to tear you down and break you down. May the Lord continue to bless you. Just when you think He did something… Hold up He is not done yet! The blessings will continue to pour in.

---

The storms and cloudy days you may experience will have you testing your faith. God will find a way out for you from whatever you're fighting through. When fighting those battles, you'll come out with some scars, but don't let that affect your life and where you're trying to get in life and what God has planned for you. Nothing is impossible when we have God almighty by our side.

It feels good having an amazing God that can fix whatever we're going through in life. The Devil tries and tell you you're not going to make it. But continue to trust God. Some circumstances the Devil places you in will have you questioning God, but no matter the circumstances or how far your back is against the wall, our savior will come through and have the Devil mad He couldn't get his way.

---

God has been so good. He is an amazing God He deserves all the praise and worship. I pray He gives you clarity and place the Devil under your feet. As long as God has our hands, he'll lead you through that desert and storm. Trust Him as He will lead you to the right direction.

---

Don't let the Devil hold you down. Let God fight your battles and allow Him to handle it. Maintain your faith and hope. He has a miracle under your name. God is making a distinction between you and your enemies. He won't guide you to the wrong direction. He is going to detour you away from the obstacles that the Devil tries to throw at you. The Devil tested you this year but He didn't break you. There were obstacles we had to get through and God got you through.

---

God is an amazing God! While we praise God, He will take care of the battle we are facing. As we praise God our enemies will turn on themselves. That victory has already been won for you. He did not bring you this far to leave us. He is a healer and a protector.

---

Sometimes life has a way of knocking you down. The Devil tries to keep you down and out but that won't happen. We praise an amazing God that hold you down and protects you from the enemy. The Devil needs to know there is nothing He can do is going to prosper. We are going to win whatever battle we are facing and come out on top.

---

You're not the only one fighting the battles you're fighting; God is right there fighting it with you. There's power in a prayer. Don't lose your faith because someone else doesn't believe in what you believe in. Live your life on how you want to live your life and have faith on what God is doing for you.

---

We serve an amazing God. God is not done blessing you. He is still not done with transforming you. The Devil doesn't like that. Continue having faith and believing in the power of the Prayer. Cherish life and the people in it. Cherish the moments that you share.

---

He's able! Trust and believe He is capable of getting you out of these circumstances. He is an amazing God! The Devil will try to say you won't overcome obstacles, but we serve a faithful God that will guide you out of anything and everything. These troubles don't last, stay strong and have faith.

---

Don't allow this moment to determine who you worship. The Devil can't do what God can do for you. Don't let these times break you down, instead, let it make you stronger and your beliefs and faith stronger. What God has for you no one can take away. You can't conquer what you don't confront! Our God is bigger than us.

---

Sometimes we're not in full strength to fight our battles but God is right there holding us up helping us to fight those battles. What's supposed to kill you are only going to unlock you to come out strong. Stop putting your trust in people and things and put your trust in God.

---

No matter how big your problem is, your God is bigger. He makes a way. Thank Him for the good and the bad, he'll make a way to carry you out of the bad situation. He is the way that healing and the answers to the questions you're asking will come. Those blessings will find a way to you.

---

Don't assume God is not with you because you're going through something difficult. Difficulties don't last when you have an incredible God walking those steps with you. God is still the God that creates miracles. There is so much going on that creates fear. People are living by fear and not by faith. No matter how bad it looks God is about to turn it around.

---

Don't let the Devil trick you into thinking God doesn't want to hear from you. With all that is going on in the world, He is all we have. Don't let the enemy steer you away from continuing to having faith and praying to the awesome God we have. He'll always steer us to the right path we need to go.

---

We all have those moments when the Devil tries to hold us back and God gets us out. When we reflect, all we can say is "Only God could have done this". God is already working out the things you're worried about. Continue to have trust in Him and praise Him through it all. When you think about what He has done for you all you can say is "Thank you Jesus". All the glory and power and all the praises go to him. Life is not promised. Stay planted and stay in position.

Sometimes God will cause you to visit old enemies to get new perspectives in life. Let them talk about you let them say what they want, but they can't stop anything God wants to do in your life. Hold on to his word hold on to his presence. Devil thought He had you, thought He can take you out, but God is got you and won't let that happen. Make your mark in life and show the Devil you can make it through any storm in life.

---

Through all this pain, trails and tribulations, we must remain strong. Continue having faith and God will come through. Don't let your doubts destroy your beliefs. Our world may not feel good, but we serve a God that is good. He will lead us through that fire during our darkest nights. Our world has changed but our God has not. We serve an amazing God.

---

This is not the season to run away and be distracted by what the Devil is doing. The Lord will help you in this season to walk in wisdom. Pray the holy spirt helps you and protect you from the Devil's work. I pray you prosper through whatever the Devil is trying to tie you down from.

Our world has changed but our God has not. We serve an amazing God. Life is not promised but you have a purpose in life. The Devil couldn't take you out if He tried.

---

Even though some things might not feel right, or you might not think things are going right at this time, keep faith those struggles don't last, He didn't bring us this far not to leave us. You are more blessed than you know. If you have breath in your lungs you are blessed. Count your many blessings and see the good in life on what you're blessed with right now.

---

Glory to God for all He has done and continue to do. I pray He let his presence be known in your life and He takes away any negative energy. He is an amazing God. He has been so good. As we search for answers in this world, put all praise and worship to Him and believe in Him that He will guide you through all of the tough times.

---

We are truly grateful and blessed to see another day. Just remember He makes a way out of nothing. Don't be discouraged right now, keep having faith and keep pushing through whatever you're going through. Continue to send those praises up and watch those blessings come down. God is able! No matter what it looks like, know that our God is able. His strength and power is made perfect for our weakness. He is our way through anything! Be grateful and thankful that during times like this He give you another chance every day to wake up.

---

With all these circumstances in life, don't underestimate the power of prayer. Thank Him for what He has done and pray for what you need. The power of prayer is amazing continue to have faith. Thank Him for all his blessings, grace and mercy. Don't let this Devil win this battle keep pushing and sending those prayers up and shake that Devil off. Those blessings will eventually come down.

---

Our God is an amazing God. Our God is a healer. Our God is a mountain mover. Our God is a way maker. He will heal every stress mind and depression. He will give you peace and guidance. Don't let these times blur your vision and distract you. We serve an amazing God that will find a way and also make a way for us.

---

He'll bring you through those storms He won't leave you out there with no umbrella. Don't ever underestimate the power of prayer.

---

Don't stop battling. Once you stop the Devil will think He won, and He hasn't won this battle. Don't let the enemy hold you hostage. Keep those prayers going up, you need to worship for who God is what He has done for you. Glory be to God. God will help you wherever you are at life, regardless of the place and time. He will bring you out of it to bring you through

---

Learn how to give God glory and learn how to give Him praise. Those troubles don't last forever. While we're going through things, we're also growing through them. Continue to thank Him for grace and healing through all the suffering in more than one area in our life. It doesn't matter who is against you if God is for us.

Every time the Devil shows up, we step on his head by praying to our amazing God. There is nobody greater than him. Don't underestimate the power of prayer. He is so faithful even when we our faithless. No matter what's going on you must stay strong. Don't let the Devil get hold of your situation. Those troubles don't last, it's just a test of your faith. We may run through some roadblocks in life.

God always finds a way to detour you from those roadblocks, because we serve an almighty incredible God.

---

No matter where you're at with the story of your life it isn't over. Be strong and have faith. We serve an almighty God that has ability to rewrite our story. Our story is not done until He says so. Have patience and let Him guide you through this thing called life. With everything going on in this world you never gave up, God never gave up on you. You'll fight whatever demons you're fighting. Keep away from the negative miserable souls. Appreciate the people and the little blessings in your life.

---

Thank Him for his love, protection and his favor over us. Give glory for all He has done for us. All praise and all glory belongs to him, our father, our savior, our amazing God. No matter what's going on you got to stay strong, don't let the Devil get hold of your situation.

---

No day is promised. Life is too short not to be anything but happy. Stay positive! Praise the Lord when things are good and when things are bad. Through any battle the Devil tries to throw at you will get through and conquer. Don't let those battles you are fighting hold you down and cause you not be happy with life. Trust in the Lord he'll get you through it.

---

It's never over until God says it's over. Keep fighting until you win the battle. God will take that burden that's holding you down off your shoulders. He will heal you. The Devil was working this year, but our God was working harder, we could have lost hope but God was holding you down. Thank Him for all He has brought you through.

---

Thank Him for waking you up this morning, thank Him for all you have and what He continues to do for you.

God is an amazing God! Through these difficult times He continues to find a way to bless us. Whatever storm comes your way just don't lose faith that storm won't last forever. Keep pushing! Don't give up on whatever it is you're going through. You don't know when God is going to show up or who is going to bless you. Stay in faith! Give Him praise for brining you through, because you're still alive. He hasn't left your side. Don't let the bad moments define your faith.

---

Things might not be going your way right now but don't give up. You're blessing will come in due time. By the grace of God, you will make it through, He will bring you through whatever it is you're going through. Those trials and tribulations don't last. The Devil tried to convince you that you wouldn't make it but you did. We serve a faithful God. Why run from the Devil when He is supposed to run from us with God behind us? He is greater than our enemy. Our faith is too powerful.

---

You'll receive deliverance from anything that's holding you back. That storm can't last forever. The light will always shine bright after those stormy days. Thank Him for being awesome. He is worthy of all our praises. All glory to God for giving you the power to wake up this beautiful day. If you're alive thank the man above. You may not have all you want but you're still alive. I pray God heal you from whatever it is you're going through.

---

That burden that's holding you down will lift off you. Continue to have faith God will lead the way. After all the Devil tried to put you through, you're still standing tall and strong. Send God those daily praises for not letting you go and not letting the Devil get a hold of you. There are too many things to be grateful for in life.

---

We give Him all the praise today for being blessed to see another day. Be great!! Don't sell yourself short God created you to be great. Don't settle for anything or anyone in life you were created for greatness. Don't let the Devil hold you hostage and keep you down. All praise to the Most-High for his continuous blessings.

Whatever dark place you're in there's always light at the end. Any road blocks the enemy try to throw your way, God will find a way to detour you and have you on the right track. And the enemy can't stop what God has for you.

---

Sometimes it seems there's no way out, but there's always a way out. God reminds you He is able and telling you be strong. The God we serve has it under control and an amazing God He is, our healer our provider doesn't ever think He doesn't have it under control.

---

We can't take these days for granted when God allowed us to be blessed to wake up and see another sunrise. It's always a challenge to continue to remain faithful when things aren't going right in life. Stress can follow you anywhere. You're not alone. He's an on-time God, He may not come when you need Him but He will be right on time.

---

God will go through every storm with us. You'll beat whatever battles the Devil may be trying to place you through. There's nobody greater than our father God. We worship an incredible God that will make a way for you through those trials and tribulations.

---

Praise Him through the hard times and good times. In these times you have to stay prayed up because the Devil is working. You can't let the Devil trick you from being great. Most of you are fighting silent battles people don't know about. Continue to pray that those silent battles go away. Those stormy days you have will turn into sunshine.

www.ingramcontent.com/pod-product-compliance
Lightning Source LLC
LaVergne TN
LVHW051923060526
838201LV00060B/4152